Shooters

forty-six outrageous shots

First published in 2006
1627 Ingleton, Burnaby, BC, Canada
by

SpiceBox™
www.spicebox.ca

ISBN 1-8966-39-74-7
Designed and produced by SpiceBox™
Book design: JW Veldhoen
Package design by James Badger

First edition
Printed in China

Contents:

Introduction

Shooters, or shots, are so named because of the glass they come poured in. A shot glass contains about one and a half ounces of fluid to drink straight up, or to drink mixed. Shooters are boisterous, in your face, and designed to get you buzzed, fast!

Each shooter has its own character. Some are gripped with your hands held behind your back, some set on fire and sipped from under flames using a straw, but most are knocked back in one inebriating and delicious gulp. Layers characterize most shooters, with contrasting colors carefully poured to separate those above from below.

It takes a steady hand, and many botched efforts to get it right. Fortunately, you can always drink your screw-ups, but this will not help steady your pouring technique for the next round.

Most shooters taste good but their names are usually anything but tasteful. Considering the character of the drink, it is not very surprising that many of them come with names designed to shock, like the *Orgasm*, *Gender Bender*, or the *Horny Bull*.

Tips and Techniques

You can create shooters a few ways, by pouring liquor carefully over the back of a teaspoon allowing it to run gently down the side of the glass and settle on top of the layer below. On the other hand, you can make shooters in large quantities in a mixing jug.

In order to make the layers of color separate, you have to pour heavier liquors before lighter ones. This is not as straightforward as it might sound because drink producers rarely reveal the heaviness of their products on the label. What's more, different brands of the same drink can have different weights. One valuable clue is the alcohol content of the drink printed on the label, either as a percentage, or as alcohol by volume. Higher alcohol content means lighter gravity. Therefore, you should start with ingredients with less alcohol, and work up to the more potent ones. The recipes in this book may require that you vary the order of ingredients to get things just right — just don't forget practice makes perfect, but too much practice just makes you drunk!

Tools of the Trade

To get started, other than the set of shot glasses and pouring spouts that come with this kit, you will need a few thin teaspoons that fit comfortably into the mouth of the glass, and a cocktail shaker. Hold the teaspoon curved side up, with the tip just touching the edge of the first layer. Send the liquor over the back of the teaspoon and onto the layer below. You may find it convenient to tilt the spoon slightly, or even bend it to suit your own pouring style. With practice, you can control your pour from a healthy glug, to the tiniest trickle.

Some mixed shooters need to be shaken and strained, which makes a cocktail shaker a handy tool to include in your arsenal. A medicine dropper is useful for adding small drops of color to the surface of a creamy drink. You can add a heart to a Valentine's Day shooter, or golden spots to a *Ginger Tom Cat*. Be sure to buy a sugar shaker if you often make shooters that require a sprinkling of cinnamon, or cocoa powder. If you make shooters on a regular basis, you may like to get technical and buy a hydrometer, and a tall glass cylinder for testing the weight of each ingredient. This will tell you which liquor goes at the bottom, and which goes to the top in ascending order. It's not an essential item, but it can be fun.

The Basics

Other accessories, which you probably already have in your kitchen include: a small bowl of water for rinsing spoons between pourings, a clean towel, and a tray to stand finished drinks. It is also a good idea to wear a bartender's apron while you're experimenting in case things get out of control.

The Liquid Mix

You will need a range of alcoholic drinks of varying colors to make shooters. Your drink cabinet may already have the basics like vodka, tequila, rum, and whiskey, but you'll need to brighten those up with a few strongly colored liqueurs. Bright blue Curaçao, emerald green Crème de Menthe, dark brown Kahlua and ruby-red blackberry brandy are just a few examples. Visit your local liquor store, and pick out a few bright colors, or else choose a few recipes that you would like to try and fill your shopping cart accordingly. Consider flavor balances when designing your own shooters. If you use a sweet liqueur, top it with a layer of something bitter, or tart, to give it balance. A syrupy liqueur becomes less sweet by adding a few drops of lemon juice, or a dash of Angostura bitters. Not all the ingredients in a shooter have to be alcoholic either. A layer of lime cordial gives a nice tang twist, while fruit juices add freshness and color. You'll find a list of liquids that you'll need on the next few pages.

The Liquid Mix

type	color	taste	alchohol
amaretto	brown	almond	25-30%
advocat	cream	vanilla, brandy	15%
angostura bitters	dark pink	sweet	20-25%
black sambuca	clear, blue, green, orange, red	bitter orange	35-40%
brandy	various	various	40-60%
cointreau	amber	bitter, orange	40%
crème de cacao	clear or dark	chocolate, vanilla	25-30%
crème de menthe	deep green or clear	peppermint	30%
galliano	clear, gold	sweet	35%
gin	various	various	40%
glayva	amber	herbs, tangerine, whiskey	35%
grand marnier	various	orange, vanilla	40%
grenadine	red	pomegranate	n/a
irish cream	off white	chocolate, vanilla	15-20%

The Liquid Mix

type	color	taste	alchohol
kahlua	dark brown	coffee	25-30%
lime cordial	green	lime	n/a
pernod	clear	anise, herbs	40%
rum	clear, dark brown	caramel, molasses	various
schnapps	clear	various fruits	25-40%
southern comfort	brown	orange, peach, whiskey	25-40%
tequila	white, silver, gold	agave, bitter	40%
vodka	clear	n/a	40%
whiskey	light brown, dark brown	caramel, smoke, honey	40%

The Shot List

Mixed Shots

Blue Balls	10
Blue Bastard	12
Blue Polar Bear	14
Crimson Hotpants	16
Electric Jello	18
Fire Bomb	20
Great White Shark	22
Gigantickle	24
Hand Grenade	26
Italian Valium	28
Jamaica Dust	30

Layered Shots

Autumn Leaf	32
Bailey's Chocolate Cherry	34
Bananna Split	36
Bloody Good Shot	38
Butterball	40
B52 Classic	42
Flaming Cow	44
French Kiss	46
Horny Bull	48
Irish Monkey	50

 Mixed Shots — easy to make for large groups

 Layered Shots — require more individual attention

 Shots on the wild side — made for dramatic effect

Layered Shots

On The Wild Side

Mixed Shots

The easiest shots to make
that you can mix in a jug
for multiple pours. No
less tasty, or less potent,
but perfect for parties!

Blue Balls

Unlike the real thing, this colorfully named shooter will be
something men will actually enjoy. And women won't have
any complaints either.

Mix together equal quantities of **blue Curaçao**, **coconut
liqueur**, **peach schnapps and lemon juice**. Shake with
ice cubes and strain into shot glasses. Whether you're a
lightweight or heavy-hitter, anyone can enjoy this lively
shooter.

Blue Bastard

A party favorite, be sure to mix this shooter in large quantities beforehand. That way you can keep the shots coming as your guests knock 'em back.

Mix equal quantities **blueberry schnapps, clear sugar syrup, triple sec and a splash of vodka** to taste. Shake over ice and serve in shot glasses. The blueberry schnapps is what makes this shooter so good. It can be tricky to find, but it's well worth it if you do!

Blue Polar Bear

On a hot summer day, a few of these cool, minty shooters can really hit the spot — so be sure to make lots!

Place three ice cubes in a cocktail shaker and add generous helpings of **vodka and peppermint schnapps**, followed by a splash of **blue Curaçao**. Shake and serve in shot glasses.

Crimson Hotpants

It's not hard to guess how this shooter got its name.
A sensual drink, it slips down nice and slow.

Just mix equal parts of **Jägermeister and blackberry brandy**. Pour into a shot glass and let the silky smoothness seduce you.

Electric Jello

If you plan ahead you can combine dessert and after dinner drinks with this novel shooter. Prepare jello as usual, but replace the **cold water with vodka**. Pour into shot glasses and leave them overnight in the fridge. Remember, vodka requires a slightly lower temperature than water. Serve after jello is set. No need for spoons — you can just suck the jello out directly from the glass.

Fire Bomb

Anyone who's ever tried one of these babies knows exactly where the name comes from. When you mix Tabasco sauce with three different kinds of hard liquor, you get the stuff that college dares are made from.

One part **vodka**, one part **tequila**, one part **Jack Daniel's** and a generous dash of **tabasco sauce**. You might want to have a chaser of iced water standing by, but then it's more impressive if you just shrug it off.

Great White Shark

The unusual mix of hot and cold is what gives this shooter its unique feel. Take care – this one's got bite!

Pour a generous helping of **tequila** and a couple of dashes of **tabasco sauce** over ice cubes, shake and strain into a shot glass. Open your jaws and shoot it down.

Gigantickle

This is a tasty drink that can be served as a mixed shooter, layered shooter or, with more orange juice in the mix, as a cocktail. Versatility is good thing!

Mix equal parts of **Southern Comfort, raspberry liqueur and fresh orange juice**. Shake with ice cubes and pour into shot glasses. For a layered shooter, start with the OJ, then add raspberry liqueur, followed by Southern Comfort. Now that hits the spot!

Hand Grenade

This shooter pays homage to the gangster days when hand grenades were called 'pineapples.'

You'll need a **fresh pineapple** and equal parts **vodka and lemon-lime soda.** Cut the pineapple into strips and soak them in the vodka mix in the fridge overnight. To serve, stand a pineapple strip in a shot glass and top it up with the vodka mixture. To fire, grip the pineapple 'pin' between the teeth, pull it out and chomp it down, following it up with the rest.

Italian Valium

The Italians consider this drink to be very calming — hence the name. Sometimes it takes a few to get going though...

Just mix two parts of Amaretto with one part gin. Stir well. Serve in a shot glass. Take it back in one go and wait for the calmness to settle over you

Jamaica Dust

If you can't afford to go on a Caribbean vacation, there's always this sweet, spicy drink!

Stir together equal parts of **white rum**, **pineapple juice and coconut liqueur**. Pour into a shot glass and dust with a generous topping of cinnamon.

Layered Shots

A little more complicated to construct, layered shots require pouring lighter liquids onto heavier ones.

Autumn Leaf

It's okay if the colors end up blending a little with this layered drink. It just gives it the color transition of a true autumn leaf anyway — from green, through gold to autumn brown.

Start with a layer of **green crème de menthe**, slide a layer of **sweet Galliano on top**, then add a layer of **dark brandy**. Finish it off with a sprinkling of nutmeg.

Bailey's Chocolate Cherry

This is a popular layered shooter that is also easy to build.

Start with a layer of **red grenadine** syrup for sweetness and color, slip on a layer of **Kahlua** and top with a rich layer of **Irish Cream**. It tastes as good as it looks!

Banana Split

If you liked this dessert when you were a kid, you're sure to love this adult version!

Start with one layer of **banana liqueur**, add a layer of **vodka**, and top with a generous layer of **Irish Cream**. Garnish with a juicy maraschino cherry. Yum!

Bloody Good Shot

This is the shooter version of the Bloody Mary. Ready, aim...

Fill one-third of a shot glass with **lemon juice**. Slide on an equal layer of **tomato juice**, trying to keep the two separate. Next slip an equal layer of **vodka** onto the juice, and float a few drops of **Worcestershire sauce** on top. Now that's good shootin'!

Butterball

Here's a really creamy drink that tastes a lot like those rich, butterscotch candies. Take one part **Irish Cream**, **one part strong, cold coffee, and one part butterscotch schnapps**.

Pour them carefully and separately into a shot glass to create a swirled effect, rather than making layers.

B52 Classic

Every bartender knows this how to make this shooter. One taste of this creamy sensation and you'll know why it's so popular.

Pour one-third of a shot glass of **Kahlua** and gently slip an equal amount of **Irish Cream** on top of it. Finally fill the glass with a layer of **Grand Marnier**. You don't have to be a bartender to make this favorite.

Flaming Cow

Straight Jack Daniel's is a bit much for some, but a little milk can put out that fire.

Place a layer of **cold milk** in a shot glass, then slide on a generous layer of **Jack Daniel's**. Moooo!

French Kiss

Everyone always remembers their first French kiss. Slide this one through your lips and enjoy the memory.

Start with a layer of **dark crème de cacao**, then slide **Irish Cream** onto it and finally, top up with **Amaretto**. Now give it a good satisfying slurp!

Horny Bull

A strong shooter with a bitter zing – nothing gets in the way of a Horny Bull!

Start with a shot of **vodka**, slip some **tequila** on top and finish with a topping of **white rum**. Add a few drops of Angostura bitters on top for a colorful finishing touch. Since all the ingredients are clear, you don't have to worry if they don't stay neatly layered.

Irish Monkey

This creamy banana shooter always goes down well so have a few shots of this jungle juice standing by in the fridge.

Start with a layer of clear **banana liqueur** and slide a layer of **Irish Cream** on top, keeping the layers cleanly separate. If you're feeling very creative, a couple of drops of **crème de menthe** on top add a tropical look.

Let's Tango

If you make this one right, the strong rum and licorice flavors dance together seamlessly to a citrus Latin beat.

Start with a layer of **Black Sambuca**, add a layer of **white rum** and top with a layer of **triple sec**. No rose is necessary in this little number.

Melon Ball

Here's a pleasant fruity shooter that won't embarrass your mom with the name.

Pour a layer of **vodka** into a shot glass, slide a layer of **Midori melon liqueur** onto it and top it with a layer of **fresh pineapple juice**. Great for people of love coolers and other sweet, non-threatening drinks.

Mudslide

This shooter tastes great even if it mixes up a bit. Layered or not, it's always muddy when it slides down.

Start with a layer of **Kahlua**, slip a layer of **Irish Cream** on top and finish with a thin layer of **vodka**, trickled on really slowly to prevent mixing.

Orgasm

There's nothing like offering an orgasm to someone to strike up a conversation. And it's a quickie to make too.

Start with a half glass of **tequila** and add an equal amount of **Irish Cream**. Whether it stays separate, or merges into a creamy blend, the result is orgasmic!

Original Sin

This shooter not only looks tempting with its emerald glow, it also goes down like a creamy mint candy.

Start with a layer of **crème de menthe and slide a layer of Irish Cream** on top. Don't forget to share!

Patti's Passion

Whoever Patti was, she sure left an impression on one shooter-maker!

This drink consists of a layer of **Kahlua and a second one of Irish Cream**. For the full effect, knock it back without using your hands. Just cover the glass with your mouth, tip your head back and swallow.

Ruby Red

A refreshing little pick-me-up that can be merged or made to look stunning with very careful layering.

Start with a layer of cranberry juice, float a generous layer of **vodka on top** and finish with a few drops of fresh lemon juice to add some bite.

Russian Candy

Straight vodka is like a slap in the face, but this sugary shooter sweetens the deal.

Start with **vodka**, slide a layer of **peach schnapps** on top and finally dribble a **little grenadine syrup** over the top. The red syrup will slide down the sides of the glass for an attractive swirling effect.

Satan's Mouthwash

Cure yourself of all pure thoughts by holding this shot in your mouth awhile before swallowing!

Start with a layer of **Black Sambuca**, and top it with an equal layer of **Jack Daniel's**. You can also swirl them together for a dramatic effect.

Twister

When nicely layered, you'll taste the three distinct flavors as they swirl down your throat.

Start with a layer of **Southern Comfort**, slip a layer of **tequila** on top of that and end with a layer of **vodka**. Take your time with this one — if you let it slide down your throat slowly, you'll be well rewarded.

Woo-Woo Shooter

Sweet and easy to drink, expect animated requests for refills.

Pour a dollop of **cranberry juice** into a shot glass and float on a layer of **peach schnapps**. **Top up carefully with vodka**. When done correctly, it has an interesting visual effect that looks like colored glass.

On The Wild Side

The following shots are all a
little out of the ordinary
and require more touch,
special ingredients,
or timing to create.

Bird Dropping

It may look like its namesake but it's a real crowd-pleaser.
The milk softens the bite of the tequila followed up by a
burst of blackberry for a nice aftertaste.

Start with a layer of **blackberry brandy or liqueur**, carefully float a layer of **tequila** on top and finish off with a layer
of cold milk. Look familiar? Depending on the brands, the
blackberry liqueur and tequila might need to change places.

Bogey

Too many of these and you might get up to some mischief
(where do you think the boogie man gets his name from?)

This consists of neat layers of **tropical coconut liqueur,
green Midori melon liqueur and yellow crème de
banana**, with a few blobs of **Irish Cream** dribbled on top.
It looks like an evil spirit contained in a shot glass, but it
tastes great.

Brain Hemorrhage

The texture of this shooter is true to its name, but it has a nice sweet finish.

Fill a glass to two-thirds with **peach schnapps** then add a layer of **Irish Cream**. Finish with a few drops of grenadine.

Bush Pig

The top layer of this fierce little drink is traditionally set alight before shooting it back, flames and all. Expect a lot of bravado from those who drink it.

Start with a layer of **vodka** then add a layer of **Amaretto** and finally a layer of **dark rum**.

Chicken Dropping

Forget the unappetizing name — this tasty shot is well worth trying! The layers of **OJ and peach schnapps** take the edge of the **Jägermeister** with a cool, fruity twang.

Start by pouring a layer of very cold (almost frozen) orange juice. Slide a layer of Jägermeister onto it and top with a carefully layered dollop of peach schnapps.

Ginger Tom Cat

This is a drink for the bartender with an artistic eye and a steady hand. Properly made, it really does take on the colors of a ruffled ginger kitten.

Start with a layer of **ginger ale**, carefully add a layer of **peach schnapps** and finally, float small drops of **Irish Cream** over the surface of the drink to create the tabby pattern. For a variation, try for stripes of Irish Cream and call it a tiger.

Glayva Sour

Pretty and refreshing, this shooter depends on the Scotch whisky-based liqueur for its unique character.

Start with a layer of fresh **lemon juice**, slip a generous layer of **Glayva** onto it and top it with a spoon of freshly whipped egg white. In the Scottish Highlands, it's reputed to ward off colds.

Gorilla Snot

This shooter gained its popularity from its repulsive name. It sure is fun to order though.

Carefully layer green **Midori melon liqueur** then **yellow crème de banana** and add a good dribble of **yellow Advokaat on top**. It looks disgusting but has a nice tropical flavor.

Gender Bender

Highly alcoholic, you might feel a tad experimental after knocking one of these back. True to the name, when you make it right, this shooter has a colorful character.

Carefully layer **blue Curaçao**, **Jack Daniel's**, **dark rum and Irish Cream**. You may need to vary the order depending on the brands involved, as alcohol content and weight differ from brand to brand.

Hot Mexican

The act of making and drinking this shooter is a fiesta on its own.

You'll need half a glass of beer to start and a slice of fresh lime standing by. In a shot glass, mix equal parts of **tequila and white rum**. Light the top and drop it quickly into the beer glass. Drink it down all at once. Olé!

Jellyfish

This shooter presents quite a challenge for the bartender, while the drinker reaps the sweet rewards.

Start by pouring a layer of **dark crème do cacao into the glass and slip a shot of Amaretto** onto it, keeping the division clear. Slide **Irish Cream** onto that and carefully decorate with a few drops of grenadine syrup.

Squashed Frog

Unsurprisingly, this shooter was named for its gruesome appearance. Sweet and tangy, it's not hard to look past its exterior.

Start with a deep layer of **Advokaat liqueur**, slip on the smaller layer of **crème de menthe** and trickle a swirl of **grenadine** over the top. Ribbit...Ribbit.... SPLAT!

Suitcase

You'll be packing your mouth with this adventurous shooter.

Fill one shot glass with **Jack Daniel's** and another with **passionfruit cordial**. Swish the passionfruit cordial around in your mouth as long as you can, then add the Jack Daniel's without swallowing. Swish some more, then gulp it back. You could substitute the passionfruit with lime cordial and call it a briefcase.

Tequila Smash

Here's a frisky little shooter that can really get the party started!

Layer the bottom of the shot glass with **tequila and carefully top it up with lemon-lime soda** or any clear fizzy drink. Slap a hand over the top and slam it down on the bar counter to get the shooter fizzing. Shoot it back in one gulp, gas and all. If you burp within ten seconds, you have to do another one. Try it with raspberry soda or come up with your own variations.